# OBJECT TALKS

## from
# Animals
# Kids Love

### VERNA KOKMEYER

**Standard**
PUBLISHING
*Bringing The Word to Life™*

Cincinnati, Ohio

## DEDICATION

To Leona, a mentor whose enthusiasm inspires me
to serve God by living and writing joyfully. Thank you!

**OBJECT TALKS** from Animals Kids Love

Standard Publishing, Cincinnati, Ohio.
A division of Standex International Corporation.

© 2004 Verna L. Kokmeyer
All rights reserved.
Printed in the United States of America.

Cover design by Malwitz Design
Edited by Christine Spence

11  10  09  08  07  06          7  6  5  4  3
ISBN 0-7847-1600-5

# CONTENTS

# MAMA DOES BEST

**Theme:** faithfulness

**Object:** alligator

**Materials:** box of tissues

**Scripture:** Philippians 1:3-6
"Being confident of this, that he who began a good work in you will carry it on to completion" (v. 6).

## ANIMAL ANTICS

Alligators are not my favorite animals. In fact, they give me the creeps. On a warm summer night, they seem to be the kind of an animal who might sneak up on me and put his huge mouth around my leg. Alligators have big teeth. I doubt I could get away from one. I'm glad there are no gators in Michigan. (*Substitute your state or change to I wish there were no . . .*)

Never in my wildest imagination would I think a creepy, crawly alligator would be a good mom. Most reptiles lay eggs and take off. Turtles make holes for their eggs and then leave on vacation. Tiny turtles have to dig out of the dirt nest and make their way to the water all by themselves. I can't imagine how the little ones do it. Most mother snakes leave their eggs and go immediately back to scaring people. Mother alligator is different. She uses her mouth and feet to make a nice place for her babies. Yuck—I wouldn't want to move mud with my mouth, but she doesn't seem to mind. Ma gator makes a mound of mud and weeds and lays her eggs in a hole she scoops out on top. She then carefully covers the hole. Mom alligator can lay eggs for about fifty babies—more than enough reason for her to run away quickly. Instead this mom hangs around for about eight weeks, just waiting for her babies to hatch.

I imagine that one day after she has been patiently lying around, she hears some rustling under the mud as the little gators hatch. Creepy alligators make creepy, grunting, croaking noises. Without hesitation mom uses her mouth and teeth to uncover the nest and help her little ones out. That's the kind of unselfish help we need in our lives.

That's the kind of help we get from Jesus. Like the mama alligator, he unselfishly stays in our lives, watching over us. When bad things happen to us, some people might say, "See you later, alligator." Old friends may run off to find new friends, but even after Jesus died for us, he stays to work in and through his children. I would think he'd lose patience. You might believe he would give up on us and decide he can't ever use us again. This is never true.

God continues to watch over us and will never give up. He'll be with you even after you grow up. *(Read the Scripture.)*

Mama alligators are faithful. We can depend on the Lord to be faithful too. He will keep using us to work for him.

## CARE AND FEEDING

How has God showed his care for you? *(Gave parents to love us, provided friends, a home, sent Jesus to die for us.)*

## ADOPTING AN ALLIGATOR

When I sneeze, I need a tissue to wipe my nose. When the meat slips out of my burger and on me, I need a tissue. When someone cuts a finger, I share a tissue. I'm giving each of you a tissue. It's not for a sneeze, dropped dinner, or a cut finger. A tissue is always a big help, and it can remind you that God is always close to help you serve him and others.

**PRAYER:** God, we thank you for faithful care. In Jesus' name, amen.

# TWEET ANIMALS

**Theme:** worry

**Object:** birds

**Materials:** snack bags of M&Ms candies, self-stick labels, marker

**Scripture:** Luke 12:22-31
"And how much more valuable you are than birds! . . .
Who of you by worrying can add a single hour to his life?

Since you cannot do this very little thing, why do you worry about the rest? . . . But seek his kingdom, and these things will be given to you as well" (vv. 24-26, 31).

## ANIMAL ANTICS

I combed my hair before I came here today. Did you? (*Pause for the answer.*) I also checked my clothes to make sure I'd hopefully look as good as everyone else. I don't want people to stare at me, so I make sure I wear clothes like others wear. That's not easy. I worry that I have the right brands of jeans and the most popular pair of shoes. I buy the shampoo advertised on the television, because it says it will make my hair look beautiful to others. (*Stop and primp.*) Sometimes it's much more expensive to shop for certain brands, but it's worth it if I look good.

I still worry when I look in the mirror. My hair is brown (*change to fit yourself*), but I always thought people would like me better if I were blond. I also think my nose is a little too long. (*Point at it.*) Once someone teased me about that, and now every day I put my finger on it and push hard. (*Demonstrate.*) I hope it will make my nose more like everyone else's nose. My chin seems a bit short. Do you think if I pulled (*demonstrate*) it would expand? There is just so much to worry about.

Do you believe God thinks I'm more beautiful if I use a certain shampoo, wear certain clothes, or change my hair color? Our Bible verse today is about birds. They can't change their clothes or their feathers. I bet they really worry about how they look, don't you think? (*No.*) Naw, birds don't bother with how they look. God made them beautiful, and I doubt they worry about anything.

Let's talk about the birds God created. There are all different kinds. Some are yellow; some are black. I'm sure you've seen a robin with a beautiful red tummy. Some have long beaks like the hummingbird, while others have short beaks. I smile when I see a bird with very long legs or when I see a pheasant with a very long tail. You can tell God loves the birds and they are important to him.

God loves the pretty birds, but he loves his beautiful children much more. He made us all different, and we don't have to try to be like everyone else or to be more beautiful than everyone else. We can celebrate our differences. As children of God we should always be our best, but worrying about how we look is for the birds. Our verse tells us to be first concerned about knowing Jesus, and all else will find its place. (*Read the Scripture.*)

## CARE AND FEEDING

Why do you think many of us are concerned about our looks? (*Discuss: Because of pride, a desire to be admired, we don't want to be different than others, and so on.*)

Is how we look important to God? (*No.*)

## ADOPTING BIRDS

Today I'm giving each of you a baggie containing colored M&Ms to remind you of all of God's different, beautiful birds and children. (*Add a label with the words: Don't worry—you are valuable to God.*)

**PRAYER:** Dear Jesus, thanks for making us all beautiful in different ways. Help us to be most concerned with staying close to you. In Jesus' name, amen.

# A SINKING SOLUTION

**Theme:** obedience

**Object:** camel

**Materials:** resealable bags, sand, rocks, marker

**Scripture:** Matthew 7:24-27

"Therefore everyone who hears these words of mine and puts them into practice is like a wise man who built his house on the rock" (v. 24).

## ANIMAL ANTICS

Camels are said to be crabby. Maybe that's because they live where there is a lot of sand. We know how hard it is to run in beach sand. It's hard work because our feet sink down with every step. Our shoes usually get full of sand, and that makes it even harder to move. That could make anyone crabby, especially if we have to keep hollering at friends or parents to slow down so we can catch up.

Camels should be grateful that they don't get sand in their shoes. Instead they have feet that are perfect for walking in the sand. Each foot has two big toes which spread apart with each step. The skin between their toes keeps their feet from sinking. Camels can do what they need to do and go where they need to go without getting slowed down by sinking in sand.

Just as camels are designed to avoid sinking, the Bible tells us we also have what it takes to avoid sinking when we are building our lives. *(Read the Scripture.)* What can our lives be built on that would keep a house from sinking down? If you listened to our verse, you will know this right away. *(Discuss building on rock.)* Nothing will sink into a surface made of rock. It makes sense to build a house on a rock, and it makes sense to build our lives on God's Word. When we live with Jesus as our rock, we won't sink in sin and the problems we might otherwise get stuck in. There's no need to struggle to catch up. The only way to keep from sinking is to listen to what God tells us and then obey his words.

Often we hear God through parents or others who love him and us. When we disobey a mom or dad, we are sure to get in trouble. Christians with lives built on God's Word avoid doing things that look like fun but cause us to sink deeper, doing more and more things that do not honor him. We have God's help. God gave the camel skin between his big toes to keep them above the sand, but he doesn't replace our ten toes with two big ones. I'm glad, aren't you? *(Yes.)* Instead he helps us be obedient and leads us to make good choices based on his Word. Our ten toes are more than enough to keep us from sinking into trouble when we listen and obey.

## CARE AND FEEDING

Why is it important to have lives built on Jesus Christ, the Rock? *(Staying close to Jesus keeps us safe and helps us avoid trouble.)*

How would you go about building your life on a rock? *(Read God's Word, pray, learn from parents and teachers, obey God.)*

## ADOPTING A CAMEL

As a reminder of how important it is to have lives built on a rock, I'm giving you each a baggie with small rock in some sand. *(The rock should be just large enough to write "Matthew 7:24" on it. Have the children learn the verse so they can repeat it when reminded by their rocks.)*

**PRAYER:** Lord, help us obey and build lives on you, our rock. In Jesus' name, amen.

# A PURRFECT SECRET

**Theme:** contentment

**Object:** cat

**Materials:** paper cups

**Scripture:** Philippians 4:10-13

"I know what it is to be in need, and I know what it is to have plenty. I have learned the secret of being content in any and every situation, whether well fed or hungry whether living in plenty or in want. I can do everything through him who gives me strength" (vv. 12, 13).

## ANIMAL ANTICS

Curl up next to a cat, and you are likely to hear a very strange noise. Cats let you know that they are contented by purring. Dogs don't purr. Do birds purr? (*No.*) Even hamsters don't purr when you cuddle them in the palm of your hand. Most cats purr. Even tiny kittens already purr while drinking their mommy's milk.

Cats can purr before or after dinner. They purr while lying on your bed or sleeping in the sunshine outside. Kittens purr while wedged between books on the bookcase, or snoozing in a box in the basement. They can purr when covered with dirt. Cats even purr when they have reason to be a little nervous. The cat doesn't purr because he is without problems. Cats have learned how to be contented—especially when someone they love is near.

Cats may have learned the lesson of being content, but not all of us know how to be content. Maybe you wanted pizza for lunch and ended up with a ham sandwich. Perhaps your mom forgot to make chocolate pudding for dinner. Much worse, you may have a friend who had something bad happen, or someone in your family is sick. It's not easy to be contented unless you know a secret.

The Bible gives us the secret of being contented. It tells us how to be happy and content no matter what is happening. Do you want me to tell you the secret? (*Look around and bend towards the kids before sharing confidently.*) The real secret of being content (*pause*) comes from knowing Jesus. The cat can purr when someone he loves is near. We can be contented because we know

Jesus is always near. Jesus promises that we can do everything through his strength. *(Read the Scripture.)*

You can be as contented as a tiny kitten. That means you don't have to be nervous or scared even if it's the first day of school. You'll be able to be okay even when other kids say mean things about you. No matter who is sick in your family —or even if you do not feel well, you can have contentment knowing God will give you strength. When everything seems to be going wrong, Christians still have Jesus Christ—someone they love—close by. That's contentment.

## CARE AND FEEDING
Think of someone in your life who is having a difficult time but may not know Jesus. Would it help them to know Jesus? *(Discuss the difference it would make: They would have a friend who loved them and was in control of everything.)*

## ADOPTING A CAT
We can only have real contentment when Jesus fills us with his Spirit. When we do not know Jesus, we are empty like this empty cup. *(Show the children an empty paper cup.)* Contentment comes from being filled. Today I'm giving you an empty cup to remind you of the friends you may have who are empty because they don't know Jesus. It's a reminder to share the secret of being contented.

**PRAYER:** Jesus, we love you. May having you in our lives give us contentment in every situation.  In Jesus' name, amen.

# SET IN HIS WAYS

**Theme:** non-conformity

**Object:** chameleon

**Materials:** a small piece of clear plastic, small squares of white poster board, marker

**Scripture:** 1 Corinthians 15:58
   "Therefore, my dear brothers, stand firm. Let nothing move you. Always give yourselves fully to the work of the Lord, because you know that your labor in the Lord is not in vain."

## ANIMAL ANTICS

Suppose after shopping for shoes to match your new clothes, you could make yourself match as well. You might choose green to match the number on your t-shirt or make your skin the same shade of blue as your new Sunday dress. Seem impossible? Maybe it is impossible for us, but not for the chameleon. The chameleon is a kind of little lizard who can change color to look like his surroundings. If he is yellow and goes to sit on a dark stick, his color could change to black. A chameleon may be white one minute, and change to green as he hangs on a leaf, waiting to shoot out his sticky tongue to catch an unsuspecting bug. The little creatures can even get blotchy or spotted. Do you think they got that idea from hunters we know, who use camouflage jackets to sneak up on animals? (*Pause and say confidentially.*) Imagine what fun it would be if you and I could match the living room carpet and sneak up on our friends.

I always thought chameleons changed color to protect themselves. You can't stomp on what you don't see. Actually, when a chameleon changes colors, it is more likely because of a change in temperature or light, or maybe something really scares the wits out of him.

Just as fear can change a chameleon, there are times when fear can change us. Suppose you are on the school bus and kids use bad words that do not honor God. Rather than asking them to stop, you get scared of how they might tease you, and you just laugh with them instead of correcting them. You might even use bad words yourself—words that you would never use otherwise. You might be with some friends in a store and decide that no one would miss one little piece of candy. You join your friends and steal rather than stand up for what you believe.

It is sometimes easier for Christians to blend in with their friends than behave as God commands. It may even seem like more fun at the time. The Bible tells us to stand firm, even when it is scary. (*Read the Scripture.*) Good behavior has rewards. If we honor God, good things will happen because of it. Other kids may want to know Jesus Christ because of your example. You won't have to worry about getting in trouble if you don't take what doesn't belong to you. Most of all, you will please God and he will bless you.

## CARE AND FEEDING

*Show the children a small piece of clear plastic. As you put it over various articles of clothing, it "changes" color, depending on what is under it. Then show them a small white piece of poster board. No matter where you put it, it remains white and different from much of what is around. Remind the children that God calls us to remain strong and serve Him everywhere, at any time.*

## ADOPTING A CHAMELEON

*Give each child a small piece of white poster board on which you have printed the words from our verse: "Stand Firm" I Corinthians 15:58.*

**PRAYER:** Lord, we belong to you. Give us the strength to stand firm always. In Jesus' name, amen.

# CHICKENED OUT

**Theme:** fear

**Object:** chicken

**Materials:** resealable bags of cotton candy or hard candies, self-stick labels, marker

**Scripture:** 2 Timothy 1:7
"For God did not give us a spirit of timidity, but a spirit of power, of love and of self-discipline."

## ANIMAL ANTICS

"You're just a chicken." Has anyone ever said that to you? It means someone thinks you are afraid to do something. He probably wants you to believe you are dumb or a coward for not doing what he wants. Comparing fear to a chicken is easy to understand. Most chickens I've met get away as soon as they can. They don't appear to be especially smart as they fly into each other trying to leave the scene. Their skin reminds me of the goose bumps I get when I'm scared.

Before another kid makes you feel bad, maybe you need to remember that chickens have some things about them that are very special. Of course we eat chicken sandwiches made out of them, but more than that, how many other birds have you seen with a bright red comb on top of their heads and a matching red thingy under their beaks? (*Not any.*) The chicken is no ordinary concoction of feathers and wings.

Chickens lay eggs. Did you know that chicken eggs are used to make some of the vaccines people are given to keep us from getting diseases? What a claim to fame! Being called a chicken isn't so bad after all. God gave chickens a purpose.

If kids call us a chicken, they usually want us to feel bad or worthless because we are afraid or unwilling to do what they suggest. Even more than the chicken, the Christian boy or girl has been given special value and purpose. God gives you and me a spirit of power and love. *(Read the Scripture.)* We can choose whether an action is good or bad for us. Then God also gives us self-discipline—we don't have to do what is wrong. You and I have the power to control our actions. That's not being chicken. That's showing God's power.

Other children are watching you. When they see you stand firm and do the right thing, they will be more confident in doing the same. When they see our actions, kids who are not Christians may want to know more about Jesus. Good things will happen because of your good behavior.

God made us special like the chicken. I'm glad I don't have to look like the chicken with something bright on my head or hanging from my chin. Instead, he makes me smart and gives me confidence to make good choices that honor him every day.

## CARE AND FEEDING

It isn't easy to be teased or picked on. How does it help to know that Jesus gives us power? (*We don't have to lose our temper. We can remember that the teasing is not about anything true. Also, we're not alone, even when our friends are not with us. We do not have to do what they want. God gives us power.*)

## ADOPTING A CHICKEN

Our fear can dissolve when we know Jesus is with us. This candy illustrates what can happen to our fear. (*Purchase some cotton candy or hard candy and divide it in baggie portions so you can give some to each child. A label can be added with the words: God gives us a spirit of power, of love and of self-discipline.*)

**PRAYER:** Lord, you made us special. Remind us that you will always give us help and strength. May our behavior always please you. In Jesus' name, amen.

# GREEN MILK AND BEEF

**Theme:** faith

**Object:** cow

**Materials:** mustard seeds, index cards, glue, marker

**Scripture:** Matthew 17:20
> "Because you have so little faith, I tell you the truth, if you have faith as small as a mustard seed, you can say to this mountain, 'Move from here to there' and it will move. Nothing will be impossible for you."

## ANIMAL ANTICS

Do any of you drink milk? Most of us drink some milk almost every day. Why do we drink milk? (*Discuss: It tastes good, especially if we put lots of chocolate in it, and it is good for us, making us big and strong.*) So we drink milk to grow and get stronger, right? (*That's what our moms say.*) Do all of you believe that milk helps you get big and strong? (*Yes.*) Does anyone know where milk comes from? (*Cows.*)

I love to look over a field and watch cows having lunch. Cows come in all sizes and a variety of colors. There are black cows, brown cows, and often you see black and white spotted cows. I've never seen a green cow. Have you? (*No.*) Come to think of it, I've not often seen a totally white cow either. Have you? (*No.*)

There is a lot I don't understand about cows. For instance, did you know (*pause and continue more quietly*) that chocolate milk does not come from brown cows? You did? Hmmmmm. Maybe you can explain something to me. If I have it straight, a black and white cow eats brown food and green grass, and eventually he gives us white milk. Can you explain that to me? Shouldn't the milk be green? (*Give time for response.*)

I just don't understand it. It sounds like you guys don't understand it either. But yet, how many of you said you drink milk every day? Even though we don't understand how the cow can make the milk, we drink it, and it makes us grow and be stronger. That is a great example of faith.

Faith is believing something we cannot see or understand. Jesus tells us that children have more faith than many adults (Luke 10:21). Big people sometimes have to figure things out and understand everything before they believe anything. Children usually believe even what they do not completely understand. That kind of faith is important because as Christians there are some things we will never fully understand.

Our belief in God is based on faith. I don't understand how he can be with all of us at the same time. Do you? (*No.*) Can you understand how Jesus was dead and then rose from the grave to save us? (*No.*) Yet when we have faith and believe, God promises to do amazing things in and through us. We know that for him nothing is impossible. (*Read the Scripture.*)

It takes faith to understand how we get nourishment from the cow's milk. It also takes faith to accept Jesus as our Savior.

## CARE AND FEEDING
How can we prove Jesus is for real? (*Discuss: We have God's Word. Also we know how God has helped us. We all have had answers to prayer.*)

## ADOPTING A COW
Scripture tells us that if we have faith even the size of a mustard seed, nothing God wants for us will be impossible. I have a few mustard seeds for each of you. (*Purchase seeds as a spice from a grocery store. If you wish you can glue to a card with the words, "With faith, nothing is impossible."*)

**PRAYER:** Dear God, help us to have faith even when we do not understand everything. In Jesus' name, amen.

# BIG, BIGGER, BIGGEST

**Theme:** Jesus never changes

**Object:** dinosaur

**Materials:** small stones

**Scripture:** Hebrews 13:7, 8
"Jesus Christ is the same yesterday and today and forever" (v. 8).

## ANIMAL ANTICS

We are told that once upon a time huge animals roamed the earth. Do you know what animals I'm talking about? (*Dinosaurs.*) Most of you know a few things about dinosaurs. Some weighed ten times as much as a full grown elephant. You may have seen pictures of what the huge brachiosaurus might have looked like. He is reported to have been 80 feet long. If we stood under him, we wouldn't even get our hair messed up. The mean and nasty tyrannosaurus rex had teeth about six inches long. A dinosaur would not make a good pet. We've seen pictures and may even have dinosaur toys, but has anyone ever seen a dinosaur in your backyard? (*No.*) Why not? (*Dinosaurs have died out.*)

You're right, and although a lot of people have ideas, no one knows exactly why dinosaurs disappeared long ago. It's hard to imagine that such a huge, strong animal disappeared from the earth. Their meals must have all been super-sized. Maybe there wasn't enough food to go around, or perhaps changes in the weather made it impossible for them to survive.

Dinosaurs didn't live forever, but the truth is, no matter how big or strong we are, none of us will live forever either. None of us know exactly how long we will live, but we know that everyone's life will end some day. When someone we love dies, it is very sad because we know they will be missed. Death may seem like bad news, but our Bible verse today shares good news. Unlike the dinosaur that disappeared, Jesus is with us today and will be around forever. When we believe in him, we don't need to fear facing anything—even the end of our lives on earth. (*Read the Scripture.*)

Does anyone know where people who believe in Jesus go after we die? (*Heaven.*) Jesus prepares a place for us in heaven. Heaven is a wonderful place, and it makes me very happy to know that Jesus will always be with me—on earth or when I live in heaven. Even when other things are uncertain, Jesus is the same yesterday and today and forever.

There are no more dinosaurs on the earth. You'll never see one in your backyard. Dinosaurs have disappeared, but Christians will live with him forever.

## CARE AND FEEDING

How do you know if you're going to heaven? (*We are going to heaven if we have told Jesus we are sorry for our sins and accept Jesus Christ as Savior.*)

The Bible tells us that heaven is a wonderful place. What do you know about heaven? Is it a good place to be? (*Discuss: We will be able to see Jesus. There will be no more sickness or pain. We will see people that we love, and so on.*)

## ADOPTING A DINOSAUR

Few things last forever. I tried to think of something you could keep as a reminder that Jesus never changes. I finally decided to give you each a little stone. Even a stone doesn't last forever, but I hope it will help you remember our verse.

**PRAYER:** Jesus, we praise you for being the same yesterday, today, and forever. We trust you to always take good care of us on earth and in heaven. In Jesus' name, amen.

# MAN'S BEST FRIEND

**Theme:** Jesus is our friend

**Object:** dog

**Materials:** squares of construction paper, paper clips, markers, and colored pencils

**Scripture:** John 15:9-17

> "You are my friends if you do what I command. I no longer call you servants, because a servant does not know his master's business. Instead, I have called you friends, for everything that I learned from my Father I have made known to you" (vv. 14, 15).

## ANIMAL ANTICS

It has been said that a dog is man's best friend. I'm not sure why. Anyone knows that every time you sit down to watch your favorite television show, your dog needs to be let out, unless he is out and needs to come back in. When dogs are inside, they shed. If you want to look good after sitting on your couch, it is best that your pants are the same color as your dog. An outside dog has its own set of problems. Neighbors get upset if your dog makes a mess while looking for treats in their garbage or barks for you while they are trying to sleep.

Still, a lot of people have pet dogs. Dogs don't mind being seen with you, even if you have your old clothes on. A dog couldn't care less if you are having a bad hair day. A dog is never too busy to play or take a ride in your car—especially if you let him stick his head out the window. A dog can be trained to bring you your slippers, but if you need answers to your math assignment, a dog won't be a lot of help. If you want to share a problem with your dog, you can be sure he won't share your secrets with anyone.

A dog makes a pretty good friend, but it is not like the friendship offered by Jesus Christ. Jesus knows everything, the good and the bad, yet loves us more than any of our friends or family. He doesn't care how we look. That's why there are Christians of all different colors and sizes. As our friend, he goes with us everywhere.

Jesus could have provided a long list of things we have to do to be his friend. He might have commanded that our toys always be picked up or our teeth always brushed. Jesus might have said he'd only be our friend if we avoided all our other friends. Jesus commands that we obey him, but our Scripture focuses on one thing. (Read the Scripture.) His command is that we love each other. We can be a friend of Jesus if we love others as Jesus loves us.

That seems easy enough, doesn't it? (No, it's not easy to love others) Does that mean you have to love the people who are stuck up in school? (Yes.) Does it mean I have to love the teacher who always gives homework? (Yes) Sometimes loving others is not easy at all, but God promises rewards. The best reward is being his friend.

A dog isn't man's best friend. Jesus is man's best friend.

## CARE AND FEEDING
Why would you want to be a friend of Jesus? (Discuss: Unlike other friends, he can make a difference in what happens to you.)

## ADOPTING A DOG
Give each child two small pieces of colored paper. Write "Jesus" on one and a line for the child to write his name on the other. Include a paperclip for them to tie the two together. On the opposite side of both, print: "Jesus is my friend."

**PRAYER:** Lord, we thank you for being our Savior and our friend. In Jesus' name, amen.

# MEMORY GAIN

**Theme:** remembering God

**Object:** elephant

**Materials:** pieces of string

**Scripture:** Ecclesiastes 12:1
"Remember your Creator in the days of your youth."

## ANIMAL ANTICS

Elephants have a large brain. That comes as no surprise to those who know elephants are the biggest living land animals. Elephants easily tower over most other animals in the zoo. It's a no-brainer to assume elephants have big brains, but it's good to know how well they use their big brains.

Have you ever been to a circus or seen elephants perform on television? (*Pause for response.*) They have a trainer with them and it is amazing to see them obey his commands. With a teacher, elephants learn all sorts of tricks that they would never be able to do on their own. What kinds of tricks have you seen elephants do? (*Discuss.*) It's fun to watch them turn around in circles and walk forward and backwards—sometimes in rhythm to the music. I've even seen them walk on a big round barrel without falling. You probably also have seen elephants with other elephants—even younger elephants. They do great tricks together. Often you see them stand on their hind legs and form a row with their feet on each other's backs. Then you might catch a glimpse of them walking off stage in a row, with trunks hanging on to each other's tails.

Elephants are smart and can learn many commands. They have an excellent memory. It has been said that elephants rarely forget what they've learned. Our brains are probably not as large as the elephant's, but our memories still allow us to remember and follow directions. Today's verse reminds us to remember our Creator when we are young and have clear minds. (*Read the Scripture.*) Who do you suppose our "Creator" is? (*God, who made us.*) Elephants know the trainer and obey his commands. We need to know Jesus, our teacher, and obey God's commands. What kinds of things does God command us to do? (*Discuss: He commands us to love others, be kind, obey our parents, help others, and so on.*)

It is important that Christians are able to obey and serve God together. Kids can work with adults. When Christians are able to work together, they do things they couldn't do alone.

Elephants are known to remember their good and bad experiences. Too often we remember the bad things that happen to us and forget all about the good things God does for us. We can remind others about Jesus and his blessings by sharing our smile and our happiness with them.

The elephant uses his memory to entertain with the tricks he has learned. God gives us a much better memory, and he wants us to use it for much more. Today's verse is especially for kids. When you are young, God wants you to remember who made you and begin serving him.

## CARE AND FEEDING

When we remember our Creator, how does it change our lives? (*Get input—we will obey God's commands, read our Bibles and pray, work with other Christians, and so on.*)

How does it help us to have friends who are Christians? (*Discuss: They can remind each other about Jesus and serve him together.*)

## ADOPTING AN ELEPHANT

When we are trying to remember something, we are sometimes urged to tie a string around our finger. I'm giving each of you a piece of string so you can tie it around a finger to help you remember God, your creator.

**PRAYER:** God, help us to always remember that you are our creator and Lord. In Jesus' name, amen.

# NOW YOU SEE HIM

**Theme:** transformation

**Object:** frog

**Materials:** small plastic/rubber frogs from the toy section or a bait store

**Scripture:** Romans 12:2

"Don't copy the behavior and customs of this world, but let God transform you into a new person by changing the way you think. Then you will know what God wants you to do, and you will know how good and pleasing and perfect his will really is" (NLT).

## ANIMAL ANTICS

Frogs make themselves known whenever you take a hike by the lake. If you get too close, you hear a series of splashes as frogs get scared and jump into the pond. At night, you may hear frogs singing you to sleep. Frogs are cute today, but they weren't always that way.

The frog starts out as an egg which is ready for unbelievable changes. Soon the egg becomes shaped more like a football than a baseball. It hatches into something that looks like a little fish. Before long, the tadpole starts looking lumpy, and after a week you can even see an eye near one end and a tail on the other. He's also getting ready for when he will be able to breathe in air. Six weeks later you can see that the tadpole is starting to get bumps in front of the tail. By three months, little arms and legs are taking shape, and you can see a mouth to eat with. A week later, the mouth gets bigger, the tail gets smaller, and soon a frog is all you see. The frog becomes what God intended all along. We can see how great God is when we watch his plan for the frog.

Just like the frog is transformed, God transforms us. We don't need to sprout powerful legs to jump with. We were born with them. We don't get bumps that turn into arms. Most of us already have strong arms. But there is one problem. We were also born with the desire to do naughty things. As Christians who decide to live for Jesus, we must make changes in our lives.

That may mean being nice to a brother or sister who bugs you. It might mean being careful not to use bad words or to do something that will hurt another person.

While the change the frog went through is huge, it is really not as great as the change we are to go through when we come to know Jesus. Some people say they love Jesus, but don't want any changes in their life. That's not really possible. When we love Jesus, his plan includes a changed boy or girl. That is not always an instant change. Sometimes it takes much longer for us to change than it took the tadpole to become a frog. The tadpole didn't change himself. God took care of the transformation. If we are willing, he will also transform us to become what is in God's plan for us. *(Read the Scripture.)*

## CARE AND FEEDING

What kinds of things do you do just because you follow Jesus? *(Get input— spend time in prayer and Bible study, be more helpful and more loving and caring of others, and so on.)*

How has knowing Jesus changed you? *(Give examples—more willing to share, kind to others, obedient to parents, and so on.)*

## ADOPTING THE FROG

*Visit the toy department or your local bait store and purchase small rubber frogs/ tadpoles to distribute to the children. You may wish to add a string collar with a tag that reads "Be Transformed." Review what transformation means so kids can share the message when they show their frogs to others.*

**PRAYER:** Lord, may knowing you change our lives to fit your plan. In Jesus' name, amen.

# STICKING YOUR NECK OUT

**Theme:** God sees all

**Object:** giraffe

**Materials:** empty cardboard tubes, stapler, marker

**Scripture:** Proverbs 15:3
"The eyes of the Lord are everywhere, keeping watch on the wicked and the good."

## ANIMAL ANTICS

If you look at me, you'll notice I'm taller than most of you, although someday you will probably catch up. There is an animal that is much taller than either of us. Do you know what animal is very tall? (*Giraffe*) If I had a giraffe standing next to me, he would be about eighteen feet tall. That's more than three times as tall as I am. Even the giraffe's girlfriend would be about fifteen feet high—still much taller than any of us.

There are some disadvantages to being eighteen feet tall—besides not fitting through the door we used to come in here. A giraffe carries around a huge heart because it has to pump blood all the way up to his head so he can think. Imagine how hard it would be if you had a neck that long. What would your bed look like if your pillow had to be way over there (*point*) and the rest of you over here? As you can imagine, when a giraffe lies down, he has a horrible time getting up, and so he usually just sleeps standing up. Bummer.

On the other hand, a giraffe gets to eat leaves off the trees that few other animals can reach. Best of all, a giraffe can see far. It would be pretty hard to sneak up on a giraffe.

Though it is safe to say that a giraffe does not miss much of what goes on around him, the Bible tells us that God doesn't miss a single thing. (*Read the Scripture.*) He not only sees us from the outside, but he also knows what is happening inside. God sees everyone, but can still take care of each one of us.

That means he saw you take an extra chocolate chip cookie before dinner last night and also knows when you were really angry this morning and wished something bad would happen to someone.

That is kind of scary, isn't it? You might imagine that some of us who have misbehaved are really going to get it someday. Do you think God will punish us for not obeying him or thinking bad thoughts? Our Bible answers that. The giraffe has a gigantic heart, but God has an even greater love for each of us. Though he sees and knows everything we do, if we are really sorry and know Jesus Christ, he promises to forgive.

What could be better than a God who sees everything and at the same time loves us more than anyone.

## CARE AND FEEDING

Is there any way we can hide something from God? (*No.*)

How do we go about asking for forgiveness? (*We pray, saying that we are sorry and ask for forgiveness.*)

Why is it important to know Jesus Christ? (*Discuss: He loves us and only through him can we be forgiven.*)

## ADOPTING A GIRAFFE

When we look around, we are distracted by everything that is happening. God is never distracted. He loves us. This pair of pretend binoculars will remind you that God always watches over us.

*"Binoculars" can be made by cutting in half the cardboard tube inside a roll of paper towels. Staple the two half tubes together. Write on the side of one tube, "God Watches Over You."*

**PRAYER:** Thank you, Lord, for knowing all about me and still forgiving me. In Jesus' name, amen.

# FLY TOGETHER

**Theme:** encouragement

**Object:** goose

**Materials:** cut flowers (wildflowers or single carnations)

**Scripture:** Philippians 2:1-11
"Make my joy complete by being like-minded, having the same love, being one in spirit and purpose" (v. 2).

## ANIMAL ANTICS

When winter comes, some people who live in cold areas of the country move to a warmer area for a few months. They pack their stuff into a car and take off to avoid snow and freezing weather. I would expect that of people. What surprises me are all the birds who leave cold weather and fly to somewhere warmer. How do they know where to go? How can they ever find their way back home in the spring? Wouldn't you think a bird would get tired flying all that way?

In the summer, Canadian geese nest in Canada and even Alaska. Then, when it gets cold, they get together to fly to Florida or Mexico. You will recognize them when you see a group because they fly in a giant "V" formation. Some say this formation takes less energy than if they all just took off and met for lunch here or there. Others believe that this formation makes it easier to follow one leader so nobody gets lost. It has been said that geese even take turns leading the group to make it easier for the leaders. It's obvious that geese care about each other.

When one goose is injured along the way, another stays with him until he can travel. Imagine being on a long trip and getting hurt so that you couldn't go with everyone else. How scary it would be to be all alone. How much better to have a friend stay with you until you felt better.

I wish people were more like geese, don't you? Geese know what they have to do to be happy and healthy, and they work together to meet the goal. What if they argued about whether they wanted to go to Florida or Arizona? What if a couple of birds held out for Acapulco, Mexico? They could risk freezing to death while trying to agree. Some people help others only when it is convenient for them. How many people would say goodbye to all their other friends and give up their vacation to be shivering with a sick friend?

Imagine if the people in your church were like geese. Do you think geese would complain about who is going to lead? Or would they get upset if they were chosen to sit with the new kid in class?

Our Scripture tells us to have the same mind and the same purpose. That sounds a lot like geese. *(Read the Scripture.)* There is a lot we can learn from the geese.

## CARE AND FEEDING
How can you, like the goose, help someone who is not well? *(Make a visit to the hospital, rest home, or to someone who is confined to their home.)*

What ways can you be supportive of your leader? *(Get children's input as to how they can help their leaders at school or at their church. Include behaving in class, participating in activities, and just being a good follower.)*

## ADOPTING A GOOSE
Geese support each other as they live together in nature. Look for some flowers you might give to a teacher at school or at church. Even some weeds have pretty flowers that can be shared. Let the leader know that you are sharing the flowers because you appreciate what they have done for you.

**PRAYER:** Thank you, Lord, for the opportunity to serve you with other Christians. May we always love and support each other. In Jesus' name, amen.

# TUBING FURBALL

**Theme:** guidance

**Object:** hamster

**Materials:** construction paper, scissors, brads, marker

**Scripture:** Psalm 16:11
"You have made known to me the path of life; you will fill me with joy in your presence, with eternal pleasures at your right hand."

## ANIMAL ANTICS

Many kids are happy to have a hamster for a pet. Does anyone have a hamster or know someone who does? (*Pause.*) Most pet stores sell hamsters. The cute balls of fur fit in the palm of your hand and are usually quite tame, although some of my friends have had some pretty wild pet hamsters.

Some kids have huge mazes of plastic tunnels they have put together for their hamsters. Have you ever seen a hamster maze? (*Get input.*) The hamster may have a square plastic box he lives in, but you can watch him through clear plastic tubes as he goes to other places. He might go through a tube to the left and end up in an area where he can run on a little round exercise wheel. He could then climb a tube to a lookout tower or go back down a little slide. It's fun to watch a hamster go though all the paths his owner has made for him. Sometimes a hamster is put inside a clear plastic ball. The hamster can safely run all over the house inside the ball. Even the family cat can't pounce on him.

The pet hamster can never be really free. You may learn that nothing scares a mother more than a hamster on the loose at your house. Left to roam, they can make a mess similar to the dreaded mouse. It is better to have a hamster safe in the plastic tunnels or ball provided for him.

Like the hamster often has paths, our lives have a path provided by our master in heaven. Fortunately, God doesn't make us stay in giant plastic tubes like the ones we see in restaurant playlands. (*Read the Scripture.*) People have choices about which way to go and what things to do. Some things we choose are good for us but others are dangerous. Don't depend on good guesses. It is best to ask God to guide. How can God guide us? (*The map he gives is our Bible.*) The Bible is full of everything we need to tell us which direction to go and how to choose our activities.

Just as you or a friend may have put together trails for a hamster, God's hand laid out a path for each of us. A hamster has fun while he scurries around in the tubes designed for him. You can almost see a smile on his face as he chooses to exercise on his tiny treadmill. If we discover and follow God's path for each of our lives, we will also have fun.

## CARE AND FEEDING

We are not in a plastic tube. Is it better to pick our own path or one God has planned for us? (*We often choose what gets us into trouble, but God knows what makes us happy.*)

Suppose we somehow get off the right path? Is it possible to get back on? (*Discuss: God forgives our sins.*)

## ADOPTING A HAMSTER

Today I'm giving you a pretend compass. (*Make from a circle of construction paper. Add a dial attached with a small brad. Include Scripture and directions on the dial—north, south, east and west.*) The words on your compass will help you remember our lesson: "God shows me the path of life."

**PRAYER:** Dear God, serving you makes us happy. Please guide our paths. In Jesus' name, amen.

# FEET FOR LIFE

**Theme:** God's Word

**Object:** horse

**Materials:** poster board, shoelaces, scissors, marker

**Scripture:** Ephesians 6:11-20
"For shoes, put on the peace that comes from the Good News, so that you will be fully prepared" (v. 15, NLT).

## ANIMAL ANTICS

Listen, and tell me what kind of animal makes this kind of sound when he walks. (*Make the clucking noise with your tongue that sounds like a horse walking.*) Most of us recognize what a horse sounds like when he is walking. More often you will find horses running. (*Cluck faster.*) The big muscles in his upper leg and long, thin lower legs make the horse perfect for moving fast and working with you.

A horse's foot has a single toe covered with a strong hard hoof. Often hoofs pick up dirt and stones. If a stone stays caught in the hoof, it could make the horse's foot very sore. People who love horses help by checking their horses' feet and cleaning the hoofs every day. If I were a horse, I'd sure be thankful for that, wouldn't you? (*Yes.*)

A horse often has special shoes to protect him from sore feet and also to prepare him for work. Horseshoes protect the hoofs of horses that run or walk on hard roads. Race horses wear very light shoes. It would be hard for them to run fast in heavy shoes, wouldn't it? There are special shoes with cleats for the horse needing to walk on narrow mountain trails or slippery, icy roads.

Just as a horse's shoes prepare him to do his work, God gives us his Word to prepare us for the work he plans for us. *(Read the Scripture.)* Our job is to tell others about Jesus. Knowing Scripture makes sharing easier. When people ask us questions, we can point them to verses in the Bible that give answers. Like not taking care of a horse's hoofs may lead to problems, not knowing God's Word can lead to pain and frustration for us.

Horses are made to run. Our excitement about Jesus makes us want to share whenever we meet someone new. It's important because the Bible tells us that no one knows when Christ will return for those who know him. We want everyone to be ready.

There are other ways we can prepare for the work God has for us. We can invite friends who do not know Jesus to join us at church or Sunday-school events. As we get older, preparation might mean going to a certain college, or learning a different language to share with people in a different country.

Horses are prepared to share good work. We need to be prepared to share good news.

## CARE AND FEEDING
Our verse also refers to the Bible as "Good News." What makes God's Word "Good News"? *(Jesus died to save us from our sins—good news for everyone.)*

How can we help others share Jesus Christ? *(Pray for others who share including our friends, pastors, and missionaries. Give money to those who need it in their ministry.)*

## ADOPTING A HORSE
*Make an imprint of the bottom of your shoe as a pattern. After cutting out a "shoe" for each child, punch two rows of three holes and provide a lace for children to use with the shoe. Review how feet must be prepared not just with shoes, but also with knowing God's Word. Print on each shoe the Scripture verse from Ephesians 6:15.*

**PRAYER:** Lord, help us prepare to share your good news. In Jesus' name, amen.

# THE SOUND OF JOY

**Theme:** joy

**Object:** hyena

**Materials:** fun-sized Snickers candy bars

**Scripture:** I Thessalonians 5:16-18
"Be joyful always; pray continually; give thanks in all circumstances, for this is God's will for you in Christ Jesus."

## ANIMAL ANTICS

Few of us have ever seen a real live hyena. Most of us wouldn't want to. Hyenas may look a bit like a dog, but coming face to face with a hyena would be a lot scarier. They have strong, sharp teeth used to eat other animals. I'd be afraid if they couldn't catch an animal, they might catch me.

As far as I can figure, a hyena has only one claim to fame. While other animals chirp, meow, or even honk, the hyena's howl sounds like laughter. In fact, the spotted hyena is also sometimes called a laughing hyena. Some people who have very loud laughs are sometimes teased that they laugh like a hyena.

If I could have only one claim to fame—one thing that people would remember me for—I might pick laughter. Have you ever noticed that people are attracted to the sound of laughter? In a restaurant, if you hear a group laugh, it is hard not to turn and check it out. When you see happy people, it makes you want to smile with them.

I would think making people happy would be a very special gift. There are a lot of people who are sick and in hospitals. How important it would be that someone could share laughter with them. Some people have had bad things happen to them. They need to hear the sound of laughter. Some kids feel very lonesome. Being able to laugh with you and your friends would make them feel less alone.

It pleases God when we are full of joy. *(Read the Scripture.)* Christians have the most wonderful reason to be joyful. We have God to take care of us. Even though the events in our lives do not always make us happy, we can still be full of joy. There is a deep sense of joy that comes from knowing we belong to Jesus and that he is in control of everything. You and I can rest because nothing will happen to us that God will not see us through. Knowing that, we can always be joyful in serving him.

Look around you. Find kids and adults who do not have the happiness that comes from knowing Jesus. Bring them along to church or Sunday school. Take time to tell them how they can invite Jesus to come into their lives.

You can make a difference by sharing the joy of knowing Jesus. The real one who makes a difference is Jesus Christ. He can bring laughter and joy. The hyena makes the sound of laughter, but with Jesus in our hearts, we will have his gift of deep and lasting joy.

## CARE AND FEEDING

What reasons do Christians have to be happy? (*Discuss. As ideas are shared, remind the children that everything we have or are able to do is a gift from God.*)

If someone doesn't know Jesus Christ, how can they get Christian joy? (*A person can ask God to forgive him and accept Jesus as his Savior.*)

## ADOPTING A HYENA

*Share the joy. Give each child a fun-sized candy bar—preferably Snickers.*

**PRAYER:** Lord, help each of us to serve you with joy. Thank you for the gift of happiness. May we share the gift of happiness with others. In Jesus' name, amen.

# HOPPIN' CARE

**Theme:** care

**Object:** kangaroo

**Materials:** resealable bags, cards, marker

**Scripture:** Isaiah 46:4
"I will carry you; I will sustain you and I will rescue you."

## ANIMAL ANTICS

The actions of the red kangaroo will blow you away. Mother kangaroo takes very good card of her baby. A baby kangaroo, called a joey, is only about the size of your thumb. Right after the baby is born, he crawls up the hair on his mommy's tummy until he finds her pouch. Inside his mom's pouch he feels warm and safe. There his eyes and ears and even his strong hind legs finish developing. There's even a place inside the pouch to get a drink when the joey is hungry.

When he is about six months old—just about the time you were beginning to sit up—a baby kangaroo peeks outside the pouch from time to time for a breath of fresh air. You can imagine what would happen if some other animal came along to scare the baby. Quick as a flash the joey would hide back in his mom's pouch. A few months later he is much stronger, and it is safe for him to jump around on his own. Then, almost immediately, his mom has another little baby to take his place.

Can you imagine how warm and safe a little joey must feel in his mom's pouch? Our Scripture today tells us that we can also feel warm and safe. *(Read the Scripture.)* When we know Jesus, he promises to safely carry us. Like the mommy Kangaroo, he's even there to rescue us when we are scared.

When we can't see God, we may forget he's close by. We may be afraid when bad things happen, but Jesus gives spiritual food in the form of Bible verses to remind us that he's always there. God gives us people to help us do things kids have a hard time doing by themselves. Adults who love us provide a warm, safe place to live. They give us food to eat and clothes to wear. They make sure we go to school so we will learn what we need to know.

Someday we will outgrow our need for total care by our moms and dads, but we will never outgrow our need God's care. Our Lord will never replace us with anyone else, for he loves all his children equally. Even when we are strong enough to walk around without anyone's help, God sticks around to protect those who belong to him.

Jesus carries us forever. You can be glad that you are a Christian child, instead of a red kangaroo.

## CARE AND FEEDING

Give some times when it is especially good to know that God carries us. (*Discuss: It is good when we are lonesome, when we lose something or someone special, when we don't have things we need, and so on.*)

Why is God able to rescue, when others can not help? (*God loves us more than anyone else. He alone has the power to make a difference in our lives.*)

## ADOPTING A KANGAROO

A resealable baggie can be sealed tight to keep what is inside from falling out. The baggie also protects something special from anything dirty on the outside. (*Write "He will carry you" on a small card and place it inside a closed sandwich size baggie.*) Remember that God seals us away from a world full of cares and never will let us fall.

**PRAYER:** Lord, we praise and thank you for rescuing us from sin. Surround us with your love. In Jesus' name, amen.

# FOLLOW THE LEADER

**Theme:** Jesus the shepherd

**Object:** sheep

**Materials:** small squares of white fleece or cotton batting

**Scripture:** Psalm 23:1-3
> "The Lord is my shepherd, I shall not be in want. He makes me lie down in green pastures, he leads me beside quiet waters, he restores my soul."

## ANIMAL ANTICS

Sheep look really fat, don't they? The sheep living in a field usually have their big coats on. The wool they grow is valuable. After the owners clip it off, it is used to make warm, wool clothing. On a freezing cold day, you will appreciate having a cozy sweater or warm woolen mittens. With that and a bunch of other stuff they give us in the process, sheep are important animals. They are valuable to their owners.

Wild sheep are said to be spunky and independent, but even wild sheep live close to friends. The sheep we see today live with other sheep in a big field or fenced in pasture. Often you see them just standing there chewing their cuds. Sometimes they eat the grass so close to the ground that it dies. You might get the impression sheep are not very smart. In fact, although you'd not choose one to represent your class in a spelling contest, they are not as dumb as they look or usually act. Like the rest of us, they just get a little freaked out when they get scared, and that's when they get into trouble. People who work with sheep insist that sheep recognize their faces and even know the face of the shepherd—the one they need to take care of them.

People also need a shepherd—and Jesus is the Good Shepherd. *(Read the Scripture.)* We belong to him and are valuable because he loves us. You will remember the parable of Jesus when he searched for the one lamb that got lost. That's the kind of care he has for us. His sheep loved him and even knew his voice.

Like sheep, most of us enjoy hanging out with our friends. All of us kids and adults are smart, but we don't always act very smart. We like being independent and sometimes think we don't need help from anyone. Then something will happen to scare us, or we get in some kind of trouble. It's then that we go to Jesus for help. That's when I'm glad He is here, aren't you? *(Yes.)*

Christians must recognize that Jesus is our shepherd—our leader all of the time. That's what our Scripture is all about. "The Lord is my Shepherd." If we stay close to him, he will care for us every day. He makes us relax and feel safe and good about ourselves.

Sheep need a shepherd. People need a shepherd too.

## CARE AND FEEDING

Why don't kids or adults usually ask for help until they are really scared? *(They want to do it on their own and forget that no one can. All of us need Jesus.)*

People, like sheep, might be hard to take care of, if there are a lot of them. Do you think there is ever a limit to how many people Jesus can take care of? (*No. He is God's Son and can take care of all who believe in him.*)

## ADOPTING A LAMB
*To remind the children about the lesson of the shepherd, give each child a small square of white fleece. Write "Psalm 123:1" on the back.*

**PRAYER:** Dear God, we thank you for being our Good Shepherd. Watch over us and keep us safe. In Jesus' name, amen.

# THE PROUD GROUP

**Theme:** service

**Object:** lion

**Materials:** buttons

**Scripture:** Philippians 2:1-11
   "Each of you should look not only to your own interests, but also to the interests of others" (v. 4).

## ANIMAL ANTICS
Usually a lion hangs around with a small group of lions called a pride. A pride might include as few as 12 or as many as 35 lions. There are father lions, mother lions, and baby lions, called cubs. The grown-up lions watch over the little cubs. If you've ever had a kitten, you can guess how the cubs might act. No doubt they love to chase their tails and each other. Can't you see them peeking out from behind rocks and tall weeds? I can just see the mother lion swish her tail and watch the cubs attack the hairy ball at the end.

Lions are not together every minute. Sometimes they go do their own thing. For a lion that usually means hunting. When they get together again, they've been known to rub cheeks and make it obvious that they are happy to see each other. Lions also take care of each other. Just like your mom sometimes feeds your friends, lion moms also feed each other's children. When an animal is killed for food, a lion will drag it over so that everyone can enjoy the feast. Can you imagine the growling noises a lion might make as each tries to get his share? (*Pause for reaction.*) A father lion can eat as much as 70 pounds when he pigs out. That's more than some of you weigh. Do you think there are really loud burps at the end of meals that big?

Lions live as part of a pride. Together they are happier and safer than if they were by themselves. Like the lions, Christians also form small groups. I'm sure you and your families have friends you like share time with. The adults relax while the kids play together. We also sometimes have dinner together with our friends. Lions don't want others in their territory, but God wants us to invite others to join us and teach them about Jesus. I would hope our after-dinner manners are better than lion's. None of us burp, right? (*We hope not.*)

Our Scripture tells us that we should be as concerned about what others need as we are about our own needs. (*Read the Scripture.*) I'm sure your family has given away some of the clothes you've outgrown. Maybe you've bought food for a family who may not have enough. Everything we do for others pleases God.

Lions in a pride know how important it is to help each other. It's even more important for us to help others.

## CARE AND FEEDING
Why is it important to spend time with other Christians? (*Learn from each other, take care of each other, share with each other, and so on.*)

Brainstorm together about some ways you can help others. (*Discuss: We should look for creative, caring ideas. We should turn our ideas into action.*)

## ADOPTING A LION
God wants us to work together to care for each other. (*Give each child a button. Remind the children that a button doesn't work without a hole to put it through.*) The hole or the button is worthless by themselves. When they are used together on a coat, they help keep us warm and comfortable.

**PRAYER:** Lord, thank you for giving us a group of people to be a part of. Help us to love and encourage each other and do what we could not do alone. In Jesus' name, amen.

# MONKEY SEE, MONKEY DO

**Theme:** sharing burdens

**Object:** monkey

**Materials:** chocolate kisses, narrow strips of paper, pen

**Scripture:** Ecclesiastes 4:9, 10

"Two are better than one, because they have a good return for their work: If one falls down, his friend can help him up."

## ANIMAL ANTICS

Does it seem to you that monkeys sometimes pick on each other? I don't mean the way you pick on your little brother or sister. Animals seem to really pick on each other. (*Imitate using fingers as pinchers.*) This is especially true when I watch monkeys at the zoo. To a monkey's way of thinking, it must be a way of trying to take care of each other. You really can't compare this to your mom or dad combing your hair. Baboons spend hours each day carefully cleaning a friend's fur. I've seen one baboon relax while another picks out any little thing that doesn't belong deep down in the fur. I don't want to get into what little things the baboon who is grooming finds, or what he does with them. Can you imagine what gets caught, or lives, in a monkey's fur coat? Just the taste of a bug would gross me out.

Sometimes baboons can be selfish. If you are an important leader, more time is spent grooming you, than you spend cleaning others. A boy baboon cleans a girl's fur after she is done with his, but he gets tired pretty quick. All baboons seem to like the friendly task. You can tell it makes them feel more comfortable—probably less itchy. Grooming makes every baboon happy.

The kids I know don't have fur that needs grooming, but there are lots of things all of us can do to make life more comfortable for others. You know that sometimes moms take turns bringing kids home from school. If a friend is sick, you might bring his homework home for him. Sometimes you just take some time to listen when a brother or sister is very sad. Your mom may make a dinner for a family if their mom is not feeling well.

Have you ever done something special for someone else? *(Yes.)* How did it make you feel? *(Discuss: Lead children to the fact that it makes you feel good when you give.)* Often we are as happy to give as to receive. Maybe that's why the girl baboon lets the boy baboon get by with a lot less picking.

Did you know that God wants us to share troubles and problems? When something makes a friend feel bad or someone has a problem he can't solve, God tells us to help. *(Read the Scripture.)* We need to share our problems, so others can make things easier.

Did you think baboons could teach us something? The monkey reminds us to serve others unselfishly. God wants us follow Jesus Christ and his example of unselfish giving.

## CARE AND FEEDING

Think of a ways you could help others. *(Discuss ideas for helping others with your time and resources.)*

Decide to do something very special for a friend to make life easier for them. Tell another friend so that you will be reminded of your plan.

## ADOPTING A MONKEY

*Print the words "Share each other's troubles" on thin strips of paper. Remove the narrow papers from chocolate kisses and replace with your papers. Give each child two chocolate kisses. Have each child save one and give the other to a friend.*

**PRAYER:** Lord, help us to share our problems with others and look for ways we can be of help. In Jesus' name, amen.

# TONGUES FOR THE BIRDS

**Theme:** speech

**Object:** parakeet

**Materials:** tongue depressors, marker

**Scripture:** James 3:1-10

"All kinds of animals, birds, reptiles and creatures of the sea are being tamed and have been tamed by man, but no man can tame the tongue" (vv. 7, 8).

## ANIMAL ANTICS

Does anyone here have a parakeet for a pet? Parakeets are able to do something that many other animals can not do. Do you know what it is? (*Learn to talk.*) How many have heard the talking of a parakeet or another similar bird? (*Pause for response.*) I'd love to have a talking parrot or parakeet. I never like to be interrupted to answer my telephone. If I had a parakeet, he could answer my phone for me. When I want to let others know that dinner is ready, a parakeet could fly all over the house and tell each person. A parakeet could even tell me the next morning how a television show ended, so that I could get to bed on time. With a talking bird, I'd have it made.

What do you think? Does that sound like it might work? (*No, parakeets usually have a limited number of words they use, and they just imitate what you say to them.*) Although some people insist they have a bird that carries on a conversation, usually birds only imitate words that have been repeated many times.

The other problem is that a bird only talks when he feels like talking. He only repeats words if he is in the mood. Just as often, they talk when you wish they wouldn't. There are a lot of jokes about birds who have used bad words at a time when you wish they would be quiet. You may have a tame bird, but you can never tame his tongue.

It's impossible to control a bird's speech, but it is even harder to control our own speech. Our Bible verse today is about how hard it is to be careful of what we say. *(Read the Scripture.)* Most of us don't have trouble taming our tongues on Sunday. That's the day we are in church and Sunday school. The problem comes on Monday. It's easier to slip and use bad words when we imitate others on the school bus or at school.

A parakeet says what he hears. We must be careful who we hang out with, and what we allow ourselves to hear. If we don't hear bad words, we will be much less likely to speak them. If Jesus is the one we imitate, we will speak with kindness and love to others. Our speech should reflect how much we love Jesus.

It's impossible for us to tame our tongues—only God can help us do that. We need to ask for his help so our speech will honor him. Even when you are a young person, you can commit to serving God with a tamed tongue.

## CARE AND FEEDING
Why is it important to serve God with a tamed tongue? (*The Christian's speech must honor and please God. A tamed tongue invites others to Jesus Christ.*)

## ADOPTING A PARAKEET
Today I'm going to give each of you a tongue depressor. Usually a doctor uses this tool to hold down the tongue to determine if we are in good health. Remember that our tongue must be controlled by Jesus. It indicates how healthy our relationship is with Him. (*Give each child a tongue depressor. Write on the tongue depressor, "No man can tame the tongue."*)

**PRAYER:** Dear God, may our language always honor you. In Jesus' name, amen.

# BUNNY TAILS

**Theme:** obedience

**Object:** rabbit

**Materials:** cotton balls

**Scripture:** Luke 11:28

"He replied, "'Blessed rather are those who hear the word of God and obey it.'"

## ANIMAL ANTICS

Rabbits are a riot. They come in a wide variety of sizes and colors. Some are white when the white snow covers the ground, and then when it's summer, their fur gets brown and they can hide easily in the woods. Even the funny-looking bunnies are kind of cute.

It would seem a bunny would be a perfect pet. How often does a rabbit's barking wake you up in the middle of the night? Rabbits don't chase the birds in your yard, and a pet rabbit doesn't have a shell to pull his head into when you walk by.

All the rabbits I've seen have two very big ears. Sometimes they stick straight up. Often they stick out to the side. (*Use your hands and arms straight up and then cross at the elbows to demonstrate.*) Imagine how well they must hear with such huge ears. You may have to shout at your dog or call forever before your cat shows up, but a rabbit's big ears must help him hear much better.

You already can guess what that means. A kid can teach a pet rabbit to do anything. "Go get the ball," you can shout, and he'll jump over to it and return it to you. "Clean my room," you might demand, and a rabbit's ears will pick up the sound and hop right to it.

We've all seen a rabbit do amazing tricks, haven't we? (*Most children will admit they haven't.*) You haven't? I thought with such big ears they could really hear well. (*Discuss: Hearing is not the same as obeying.*) Do you mean to tell me that a cute little bunny sometimes doesn't do what he is told? No wonder he needs a different color to hide in the woods.

It's a good thing people know how to hear and obey. When we hear a command—even though our ears are smaller than the rabbits—most of us *always* do what we are asked. (*Pause.*) Or most of the time. (*Pause.*) Or some of the time, maybe.

Did you know that God's Word has a verse about hearing and obeying? (*Read the Scripture.*) It isn't enough to hear God's commands and then ignore them to run off and do something else. When the Bible tells us to do something or act in a certain way, we must do more than just hear. We must obey.

## CARE AND FEEDING

*In the game "Simon Says," children obey only if the command is from Simon. Discuss how important it is that the commands we obey only come from God or someone to whom he gives authority, such as parents or teachers.*

How does God tell us what to do? (*The Bible, other people who love him and us, and so on.*)

Why do we find it so hard to obey? (*It's not always what we want to do at the time, but it may be what's best for us.*)

## ADOPTING A RABBIT

Whenever I see a rabbit, he's not obeying anyone. He's usually running off. All I usually see is the rabbit's tail. It reminds me that it's possible to be able to hear with very big ears without obeying. Today I'm going to give you each a little cotton ball to remind you of a bunny's tail. When you have it in your pocket, remember that God wants you to hear and obey.

**PRAYER:** Lord, we hear you speak to us. Help us obey. In Jesus' name, amen.

# FIRST DIBS

**Theme:** God provides

**Object:** raccoon

**Materials:** 2-inch squares of paper, stapler, markers and colored pencils

**Scripture:** Matthew 6:33
"But seek first his kingdom and his righteousness, and all these things will be given to you as well."

## ANIMAL ANTICS

In books or articles about the raccoon, you will read that raccoons like to eat food found by the water. They feast on delectable entrées such as shellfish or delicious frogs. You and I know better. With a black mask to protect their identity, raccoons get their food by stealing from our garbage cans. They feast on old bread, rotten fruit, and the tuna that didn't smell just right to us three days ago.

I wouldn't mind sharing my leftovers with a robbing raccoon if only they didn't have such atrocious eating manners. They never put the lid back on our garbage can, and the smell travels. Coffee grounds are sprinkled on wrappers that blow all over the neighborhood. They leave little doubt that all of the raccoons in the neighborhood get nourishment from eating my leftovers.

How many of you would like to scrounge around in garbage cans for food? Not me! None of us would want leftover secondhand food, but sometimes that's exactly what we eat. A secondhand dinner seems gross to us, but when it comes to spiritual food some of us are willing to always get it secondhand. Our moms and dads and teachers read us stories from the Bible and pray for us. All of that is very important—especially when we are young. At some point, after you learn to read, you must get the spiritual food firsthand. Some of you are old enough to read God's Word for yourself every day. It may be possible for your mom or dad to get you a children's Bible to make it easier for you to read and understand.

Even if you are not old enough to read the Bible for yourself, you can spend time in prayer every day. God loves to have us come to him in prayer. We have a lot to tell him. First of all, we can tell him how much we love him. When we have not served him as well as we had planned, we can confess that to him. Each day things happen that we can thank him for, and we can also ask for his help with the problems in our lives. Now is the best time to get in the habit of having devotions every day. When you stay close to God through reading the Bible and praying, you will know firsthand the best of his blessings. *(Read the Scripture.)*

## CARE AND FEEDING

Why is it important to read the Bible and pray? (*It is how we speak to God and how he speaks to us.*)

*Children may not know what to pray about. The older children may be able to understand a prayer "path." It will remind them what they can include in their prayers: P is for praise, A is for apology, T is for thanks, and H is when we ask for God's help. Encourage the children to set aside a time each day to spend with Jesus in prayer and/or reading the Bible.*

## ADOPTING A RACCOON

*Make each child a five-page booklet. On the cover print "Prayer Path." Put one word on each of the other pages: Praise, Apology, Thanks, and Help.*

**PRAYER:** Lord, thank you for all the blessings we can expect when we spend personal time with you. In Jesus' name, amen.

# HERE KITTY, KITTY

**Theme:** discernment

**Object:** skunk

**Materials:** packs of chewing gum

**Scripture:** Philippians 1:9-11
"And this is my prayer that you may be able to discern what is best and may be pure and blameless until the day of Christ" (vv. 9, 10).

# ANIMAL ANTICS

I wish you could have seen him. I was driving along and saw this darling animal. He was so cute. The first thing I saw was his pointed little nose sticking out in front as he hurried across the road. His coat was shiny black with a big fluffy tail. His short little legs helped him hustle across the pavement, and I got a good look at him when he went in front of the car. He was just adorable—and this is the best part of all. His little head was white on top, and the cute little nose had a tiny stripe of white running up his forehead. Come to think of it, his back also had a stripe. It kind of parted halfway down his back so you could see it on either side—whether he went from the woods to the field (*point left to right)*, or the field back to the woods (*point right to left)*. Even his tail had a white streak on it.

I was in a hurry, or I would have stopped to pet him. He looked friendly enough. I wish I knew what kind of an animal he was. I would like to get one for a pet. Do you know what animal he might have been? (*Skunk.*) A skunk! Do skunks make good pets? (*No.*) Oh, come on now. They are so cute. Why wouldn't I want one for a pet? (*Smell.*)

I'm teasing you—I know that if a skunk gets scared, he squirts out a horrible-smelling spray. You can be as far as 12 feet away, and he'll still get you. You might have thought he was already leaving, but he gets you from behind. It takes days for the smell to leave you. A skunk looks cute, but if he sprays you, you will be sorry. You will smell like a skunk for a looooong time.

There are other things in life that look good but are not good for us. Candy looks and tastes good, but too much of it isn't good for us. Other people may try to get us to try something dangerous to our health. Even if they tell us how good it will feel, don't be deceived. We may see a bracelet in a store, but be short the money to buy it. Don't be tempted. Stealing is wrong.

Christians must make good decisions if we are to stay pure. (*Read the Scripture.*) Like the bad-smelling consequences of meeting a smelly skunk, we will be sorry if we are deceived and meet up with trouble. Be careful. Judge carefully.

## CARE AND FEEDING

How can we make the right choices? (*Study God's Word and pray about decisions. Ask adults who love you and love God to help make the hard decisions.*)

## ADOPTING THE SKUNK

We could be deceived by a skunk and live with the smelly consequences. God wants none of that for us. I'm giving each of you a stick of gum to remind you not to be deceived. (*Remove all the sticks of gum from the wrappers and carefully return the foil to the inside of the paper. If you wish, you can share the gum later.*)

**PRAYER:** God, give us wisdom to make choices that will keep us close to you. In Jesus' name, amen.

# FIELD OF STRIPES

**Theme:** talents

**Object:** zebra

**Materials:** pencils with erasers

**Scripture:** 1 Corinthians 12:4-11
"There are different kinds of gifts, but the same Spirit. There are different kinds of service, but the same Lord" (vv. 4, 5).

## ANIMAL ANTICS

What's black and white and red all over? If you know the joke, you know the answer: a blushing zebra. Of course, I doubt that zebras blush, much less get embarrassed. They may have varying shades of brown and black color, but to tell you the truth, I think that if you've seen one zebra, you have seen them all.

The truth is that no two zebras are exactly alike. One zebra might have a dark line down his nose, while another has a streak just above his toes. One has stripes swirling around his tummy, while another may look like the paint ran out before his left leg was finished. Though every zebra may be a little different from all others, they all look a lot alike to me. If we were to look across a herd of zebras, I doubt if we could tell a zebra's uncle Ziggy from his brother Zaggy. Blacky looks an awful lot like Whitey. From four hoofs to one tail, I think that if you've seen one zebra, you've seen them all.

I must confess—people sometimes look the same too. Of course some have brown eyes, while others have blue. Some of us have darker or lighter skin.

Some of you have light hair and others have darker hair. Like the zebra, I'd guess some of us can run faster than others. But really, sometimes in a very large herd—or group—it's very hard to remember who is who, isn't it? Sometimes a person's face looks familiar, but I can't remember how I met them, much less their name.

We may have trouble remembering who is who, but God knows each of us. Like the zebras, he made us all uniquely different. A scientist might say that this is because our DNA molecules come together in a variety of ways. The Bible tells us that God made each of us different so we could each serve him in our own special way. (Read the Scripture.) He gave each of us talents that are very different from other kids' talents. Some of us can run fast, while others spend extra time to carefully get from one place to another. Some of you are learning to play the piano. Many children like to sing. Others like to draw pictures, while still others like to read or write for others to read. All talents are important as we serve God together.

## CARE AND FEEDING
What talents did God give you that could be used to serve God? (Have children share some of the things they do well. Don't forget to include talents not easily recognized, like not being too shy to meet new kids.)

Are there any talents you have that you are not using for God? (Discuss how some of our talents could be used.)

## ADOPTING A ZEBRA
Give each child a pencil with an eraser. Note that one end writes and the other end erases, but both parts of the pencil are important. Each boy and girl has a different talent, but like the ends of the pencil, each child has equally important talents that need to be used to glorify God.

**PRAYER:** Lord, you have made us all special. Help us to use our special gifts in a ways that will please you. In Jesus' name, amen.